MW01148105

LA DOLCE VITA

COFFEE

First published in 1999 by
New Holland Publishers (UK) Ltd
London • Cape Town • Sydney • Auckland

24 Nutford Place
London W1H 6DQ
United Kingdom

80 McKenzie Street
Cape Town 8001
South Africa

Level 1, Unit 4, 14 Aquatic Drive
Frenchs Forest, NSW 2086
Australia

Unit 1A, 218 Lake Road
Northcote
Auckland
New Zealand

10 9 8 7 6 5 4 3 2 1

ISBN 1 85974 160 6

DESIGNED AND EDITED BY
Complete Editions Ltd
40 Castelnau
London SW13 9RU

DESIGNER: Blackjacks
EDITORIAL DIRECTION: Yvonne McFarlane

Reproduction by PICA Colour Separation, Singapore
Printed and bound in Singapore by Tien Wah Press Pte Ltd

Picture Credits: Cover picture © Graham Atkins Hughes/*LIVING ETC*/IPC MAGAZINES. The publishers would like to thank CEPHAS/Don McKinnell, the Coffee News Information Bureau, Gourmet Magazine, Gevalia Kaffe, Illy Coffee Company, Lavazza Coffee Company, International Coffee Organization, Starbucks Coffee, the Coffee Board of Kenya, CEPHAS, Grapharchive and the Corcoran Collection for their assistance. Every effort has been made to identify other illustrations. Any errors or omissions will be corrected in future editions.

CONTENTS

A MOST SEDUCTIVE BEAN

The Story of Coffee

"If I can't take my coffee break
Something within me dies . . ."
FRANK LOESSER, *HOW TO SUCCEED IN BUSINESS*

Coffee was always an exotic drink and so it remains today. Smouldering passions crowd television commercials over cup after cup of rich, dark coffee, sipped wistfully on a dusty desert train journey, or savoured aboard a yacht on a romantic tropical night, until a solo cup becomes a delightful duet.

Today, the aroma and taste of a cup of coffee are enjoyed the world over, though the story of coffee begins in East Africa.

Legend has it that in the depths of Abyssinia, today's Ethiopia, sometime around the middle of the ninth century, there lived a sober goatherd called Khaldi. One day his normally lethargic goats pranced home in an agitated state. Curious at their antics, he followed them and discovered that they had been nibbling the red berries of an evergreen tree.

Khaldi decided to try some himself and was soon in a state of euphoria. In his excitement, he dashed off to broadcast his find and came upon an elderly Moslem mullah, who was depressed by his tendency to nod off during prayers.

Khaldi let him into the secret of the red berries and coffee took its first step towards becoming one of mankind's favourite pick-me-ups.

Being of a more academic frame of mind than the goatherd, the mullah experimented with the berries and eventually hit on the idea of boiling them, turning the raw fruit of the coffee tree into a fragrant and delicious beverage.

Coffee being roasted and brewed (on right)

Coffee still grows wild on the central plateau of Ethiopia, but it was across the Red Sea, in Yemen, that it became firmly established as a popular drink within a few hundred years of its discovery. From Mocha, the principal port of Yemen at that time, which gives its name to Mocha coffee, beans were shipped to wider shores: to India, Java and Venice.

At first coffee was regarded as a wonder drug and was only consumed in Yemen and Arabia on the advice of a doctor.

However, coffee was too exciting to be restricted to medical use for long. Many saw it as

An early Middle Eastern coffee-house

a brain tonic. Others credited coffee with stimulating religious visions and before long, coffee-houses had sprung up right in the heart of Mecca, the holiest city in the Islamic world.

The fashion for these coffee-houses spread northwards and reached Europe by the 17th century; according to some sources the first coffee-house in Europe was opened in Venice in 1645.

The Arabs were jealous of their discovery and refused to allow fertile coffee seed to leave their country; all seeds had to be parched or boiled. However, late in the 15th century a Moslem pilgrim from India, one Baba Budan, bound seven seeds to his torso and smuggled them out of Arabia to be planted at his hermitage near Chikamalagur in southern India. It is said that all the world's coffee flowed from these seven seeds.

There are two principal species of the coffee plant used for the commercial production of coffee: *Coffea arabica* is the one that originated in the Middle East, *Coffea robusta* originated in the Congo. *Arabica* coffee trees produce the best-quality coffee and are the most widely cultivated around the world. *Robusta* trees are hardier and can withstand greater extremes of climate than *arabica* trees; *robusta* coffee beans are the principal beans used in many instant coffees.

The Dutch were the first Europeans to enter the coffee trade. They imported coffee plants from the Malabar coast of India to their colonies in what were then called the Dutch East Indies, in present-day Indonesia.

Coffee time during the Californian Gold Rush

In 1715, Dutch coffee merchants, eager to curry favour with Louis XIV, the powerful and influential King of France (also an ardent coffee drinker), presented him with a coffee tree of his own. From that single tree millions and millions of coffee trees, including those in Central and South America, have sprung.

The first sprouts of the plant reached the French Caribbean island of Martinique in 1720, through the efforts of one of coffee's greatest heroes, Chevalier Gabriel Mathieu de Clieu.

Unable to convince the French authorities to give him some cuttings, de Clieu stole them and set sail to the French colony in the Caribbean, to begin cultivating coffee on Martinique.

On the voyage, he thwarted attempts to kill off the plants. His ship was attacked by pirates and then becalmed, causing a shortage

Gabriel de Clieu tending the first coffee tree in the French Caribbean

of water. Only one seedling survived; de Clieu bravely sharing his water ration with the lonely plant to sustain it until the spindly shoot arrived safely in Martinique.

Once planted, the seedling flourished and within 50 years there were over 20 million trees on Martinique and neighbouring islands. Sadly, de Clieu did not live to see the first harvest, but by the time of his death, his efforts had been honoured and he was placed in the pantheon of great Frenchmen alongside Antoine Parmentier, who brought the potato to France.

In 1730, the British introduced coffee to Jamaica, home of the great Blue Mountain blends, and a century-and-a-half later, the precious crop came full circle back to East Africa, when the Kenyan coffee industry was established by British planters in the 1880s.

At the same time, the French took coffee further east to Vietnam and in 1896 coffee trees were planted in Queensland, in Australia. Those seeds came from *robusta* plants growing in Brazil, now the greatest coffee producer in the world.

In the 1720s, the Emperor of Brazil had been determined to make his country part of the blossoming world of coffee. He sent his emissary, Don Francisco de Mehla Palheta, to French Guiana to obtain seeds, but, like the Arabs and Dutch before them, the French jealously guarded their treasure.

The suave and charming Don had no success with the authorities, but for the glory of Brazil, he won over the wife of the French governor. Buried in a bouquet of local flowers, she sent him the seeds and shoots from which the mighty Brazilian coffee empire has grown – a fitting story to end a brief history of this most seductive bean.

Le Vieux Garçon, *a French painting of 1885*

Growing Coffee

BEAN BOUNTIFUL

"Coffee should be black as Hell, strong as death, and as sweet as love."

TURKISH PROVERB

Coffee trees take three or four years to mature. They bear fruit in rows along their branches soon after the appearance of delicate white blossom which has a strong, jasmine fragrance.

The cherry-like fruit of the coffee berry, within which the beans, or seeds, are stored, appear green at first, gradually darkening to a rich crimson. *Arabica* berries ripen in six to eight months. *Robusta* berries take up to three months longer. This allows only one harvest a year, though Colombia and Kenya – with erratic wet and dry seasons – can have a secondary crop.

Coffee harvest times vary according to geography: those coffee-producing regions north of the Equator generally harvest their crops late in the year, while in the southern hemisphere coffee is harvested in spring. Equatorial countries are able to harvest coffee all year round.

Although there is some mechanical harvesting, plucking by hand results in better

3-01-1056
ONACO
01-1056
PRODUCTO
DE
COLOMBIA

sorted berries and does not damage the trees in the way mechanical harvesting does. Most *arabica* coffee is picked by hand.

Although yields vary from harvest to harvest, a single coffee tree usually provides only enough coffee beans in a year to fill a half-kilo (one pound) bag of ground coffee.

Two methods are used to process coffee beans once they have been picked. The most economical is the "dry" method, in which the harvested berries are spread out in the sun and raked over regularly to prevent fermentation. Once "dry" (in reality still with a small moisture content), they are stored in silos to lose their remaining moisture.

The "wet" method of processing coffee berries preserves more of the flavour of the bean. The pulp surrounding the bean is removed soon after harvesting and what remains of it is washed off

Sequence from an 18th-century German engraving of a coffee factory, showing details of the roasting process

with water. While the beans are floating in the water it is also possible to separate the small immature beans from the larger, mature ones.

After either process, the beans are dried in their parchment-like casings. They are stored in this form, as "parchment coffee", ready for shipping.

Before being exported, the coffee beans are "cured", through the removal of their parchment casings. They are then polished and sorted by size and density into six recognized grades before being offered for sale.

With the exception of the elephantine, or *maragogype*, bean, which is a large hybrid originating in Brazil, coffee beans are flat on one side and half-oval on the other.

The grading process is also the time when any black, sour, or otherwise imperfect beans are removed; failing to do so can result in the whole consignment being spoiled. Automation has been tried, but most imperfections are best spotted by sharp, human eyes.

A sequence of pictures (here and overleaf) from the 18th century showing the progress of coffee from the tree to the cup

When a consignment of beans is offered for sale, the coffee is tasted as a liquor by the roasters buying the beans. Later, they will roast them to suit their home markets; little ready-roasted coffee is produced in the country of origin, because freshly roasted coffee has such a short shelf-life.

Roasting coffee is as much an art as blending a fine wine or whisky. Complex chemical changes take place within the beans

during roasting and the roaster's expertise lies in knowing how to treat a particular bean and how long to roast it to achieve the perfect result for the desired blend.

In theory, the beans will be correctly roasted by the time they have finished moving along the screw inside a gas-fired roasting drum. Smaller specialist retailers will use a simpler drum, rotating

over a fire, with a fan to draw away fumes. The important thing is that the beans are on the move during roasting, giving an evenness of flavour and avoiding scorching.

After roasting, they are cooled quickly. And once roasted, they are packed and sent on their way, ready to be transformed into the heady brew with which so many of us begin and end the day.

THE POT OF PERFECTION

Making Coffee

"I did make coffee once, after sendin' out for instructions. But then I got otherwise involved in somethin' more interestin' and forgot to turn off the heat. Well – I never turn off the heat."

MAE WEST

Buy little and often is the best policy to adopt if you want to enjoy coffee to the full. Coffee is not something to lay down for posterity!

If you have access to a speciality shop, buy freshly roasted beans as and when you need them; simply walking into such a shop and inhaling the aroma is an experience in itself.

THE POT OF PERFECTION

For generations, London's committed coffee drinkers have frequented H. R. Higgins in Duke Street, one of the capital's leading coffee suppliers. In Paris, La Brûlerie on the Boulevard de Charonne will make up a blend to suit your taste and keep a record of the recipe for your next visit. In New York, you would be hard pressed to better Zabar's at 2245 Broadway. There, they taste and roast their own coffee which New Yorker's eagerly consume at the rate of 10,000 lbs (4,545 kg) a week!

If you really care about your coffee, buy green beans and roast them to your own taste at home. There are plenty of home roasters on the market now, but you may not think the expense/use ratio is in your favour. Much as you love coffee, you may not want your home to smell like a coffee-roaster's all the time.

One simple trick is to roast coffee beans in the oven of your kitchen cooker on a high heat, 230°C/450°F/Gas mark 8. Spread the beans evenly, preferably on a pierced baking tray like the ones sold to bake pizza. Roast for ten minutes until you hear them crack and note the change of colour. If you have previously decided what colour you want them to be, take them out when they are a shade lighter as they will continue to roast internally for another couple of minutes at least. Put them by an open window or somewhere cool to reduce the heat quickly.

If you are buying commercially produced coffee, the only sure way of discovering what you really like is to taste, taste, taste.

One of the joys of drinking coffee is devising your own blend and, if you are buying beans, a good grinder is a worthwhile investment. An old box grinder looks the part and gives the best results. Electric grinders need careful watching as your coarse-ground beans can become too fine through just a moment's inattention.

Finer grinds are best for espresso coffee; coarser grinds are better suited to filter or cafetière methods.

COFFEE EXPRESS

Speciality Coffees

"I like my coffee like my men, black and strong."
LINE FROM THE MOVIE *AIRPLANE*

After a lull in popularity in the 1970s, following the coffee-bar explosion of the late 1950s and 1960s, coffee is once again making a great breakthrough. Specialist shops, and more importantly, coffee-bars have sprung up in abundance. They offer a great range of coffees including, invariably, a speciality of the day.

The names of the brews are still linked to Italy, home of the first commercial espresso machines, which were made in Milan in the early years of this century. The most common brews are:

AMERICANO – an espresso thinned with hot water.

DOPPIO – gives you twice the amount of a standard espresso.

ESPRESSO – very strong coffee, machine-made by forcing steam through fine grounds.

Serious coffee drinking is now targeted at a younger audience, as this advertisement for Lavazza, one of Italy's leading brands, clearly demonstrates

ESPRESSO RISTRESSO – made by cutting off the machine earlier than for a regular espresso, thus making the coffee more intense and aromatic.

CAFFÈ LATTE – made by adding warmed milk to freshly brewed espresso. It can be topped, in a glass, with frothy milk and a dash of chocolate or cinnamon.

CAPPUCCINO – espresso diluted with milk. Using two-thirds milk to coffee, the milk is heated by passing steam through it, which makes it frothy. A little cocoa powder or grated chocolate may be sprinkled on top.

ESPRESSO MACCHIATO – espresso with the tiniest "mark" of milk.

LATTE MACCHIATO – vice versa, hot milk with a hint of espresso.

CAFFÉ
ESPRESSO
SERVIZIO

CAFFÈ ESPRESSO SERVIZIO

In the 1930s Francesco Illy developed a machine that forced compressed air, rather than steam, through coffee grounds. In 1945 Achille Gaggia invented the spring-powered, piston-lever machine. Both allow the greatest amount of flavour to be extracted from the grounds so quickly that the coffee produced has no time to become bitter.

ESPRESSO ROMANO – created by adding a twist of lemon!

CON PANNA – espresso with whipped cream.

MOCHA – a classic mixture of one-third espresso, one-third hot chocolate and one-third steamed milk. Go coffee crazy and top with whipped cream and a sprinkling of cocoa – sweet is best.

VARIATIONS ON A COFFEE THEME

"I have measured out my life with coffee spoons."
T. S. Eliot, "Love Song of J. Alfred Prufrock"

Coffee has made some enjoyable marriages of flavour, particularly with chocolate, and can be served in many variations.

COFFEE AND CHOCOLATE

The basic chocolate variation is usually called Mocha, but it is also served up as Caffè Borgia, Viennese Coffee, Javanese Hot Mocha and Mexican Negrita. Powdered bitter chocolate or cocoa powder make the most soothing blend. Melt the chocolate slowly, add sugar or honey to suit your taste and then stir into freshly made coffee, beating to make it frothy. Add a dash of cinnamon if you wish, to create a concoction which will make Voltaire, the French writer with a passion for coffee (he drank fifty cups a day), drool in his grave.

ICED COFFEE

This is a truly refreshing drink. The risk is to make it stronger than you would normally, especially if you are cooling it by adding ice cubes or ice-cream. It is often sold under a variety of names, from simple Iced Mocha, to Café Glacé, Refresco de Caffè and as frappés, frosts or floats.

Pure iced coffee, or Viennese Coffee, is strong, chilled coffee served with whipped cream or chilled milk.

For the more adventurous there are cold alcoholic variations. Make an Iced Coffee Cocktail by adding a strip of lemon peel and a measure of Crème de Cacao or Cognac to a jug of cold coffee.

And for those with romance in their soul, there is the infamous Café Mazagran, named at the Algerian fortress where French Foreign Legionnaires invented it, while fighting the Bedouin. Make very strong coffee, pour over ice and then add soda water to taste.

WINTER WARMERS

These include the ever-popular Irish Coffee, made with the addition of Irish whiskey and cream floating on the surface. A variation, yet to become as widespread, is to float some stiffly whipped egg whites, with a hint of vanilla essence, on the coffee.

A more unusual cup is Coffee Grog, made by adding a knob of butter, some brown sugar and a little each of ground cloves and nutmeg. This is best made with a heavy-bodied coffee and garnished with strips of orange and lemon peel.

Then there are the multitude of personal variations. If you like Calvados, add Calvados. If you like Grappa, add Grappa. Nor should you overlook the coffee liqueurs such as Jamaica's Tia Maria and Mexico's Kahlua. A dash of molasses, if to hand, enhances the aroma.

COF

FEE CORNUCOPIA

"Not instant, darling. Grind some beans. That's not proper coffee . . . that's just beans that have been cremated. I want them active with life force."

JENNIFER SAUNDERS, BRITISH COMEDIENNE AS EDINA IN THE TV SERIES *ABSOLUTELY FABULOUS*

The Turks called their coffee-houses "schools for the wise" and coffee-houses, no matter where they are, retain that sense of subtle glamour and intrigue that has been their hallmark down the ages. London's Lloyd's insurance market is just one international business centre which came into being in a coffee-house, the one where marine insurers happened to socialize.

You can be strolling through Montmartre early in the morning, hurrying through Manhattan at mid-day or enjoying a night-time saunter in Milan or Melbourne, when the irresistible smell of fresh coffee lures you into the cosy intimacy of a coffee-house.

Both the French and American Revolutions were nurtured in coffee-houses. The speeches which led to the storming of the Bastille were written in the Café Foy and Daniel Webster called Boston's Green Dragon coffee-house "the headquarters of the Revolution".

America has led the current resurgence in the fortunes of coffee as the supreme social beverage. This began in Seattle, home of Starbucks, the world's biggest chain of coffee-shops, made even bigger with their 1998 acquisition of the British-based Seattle Coffee Company, inspired by the Starbucks original.

From Turin to Tokyo, every major city has coffee-houses that take pride in perfecting the art of preparing and serving the world's most invigorating and popular beverage. Here are some of the leaders in this rapidly growing field.

AMERICA

The coffee-house tradition came naturally to America from London and the early establishments were modelled on those in London, although they were a little more serious.

Like Mr Lloyd's in the City of London, they were places where business took place and information was circulated. They incorporated meeting rooms, which were used for trials, auctions and ship sales.

But tea still ruled, until King George III's Stamp Act of 1767 increased taxes, resulting in the Boston Tea Party of

1773, when the citizens of Boston dumped the British East India tea cargoes into the harbour.

From that point, coffee became America's national drink, emotionally linked to its revolution. And so it remains. The price of one cup still buys you all the coffee you can drink. Have a nice day!

In New York, places to see and be seen include Café Tabac in the East Village, frequented by Madonna, young guns from the movie industry and the city's top models. Elaine's at 1703 2nd Avenue is another rendezvous of the stars, favoured by Woody Allen among others; his preferred table is by the cappuccino machine.

AUSTRALIA

With its cosmopolitan atmosphere, Australia, and Sydney in particular, boasts some memorable cafés. Cappuccino City in the Paddington district has established itself as a leader. On a terrace set back from showy Knox Street, Sydney's élite sip their favourite blends at Cosmopolitan. The Gelato Bar on Bondi Beach has also long been famed for its excellent coffees and mouth-watering pastries.

AUSTRIA

Viennese coffee-houses, such as Café Schwarzenberg (opposite) or Demel's on Kohlmarkt, which lure clients with their *sachertorte* and *dobostorte* to accompany their extensive range of coffees, are also homes to intellectuals and thinkers who sit in deep discussion for hours. One much-quoted anecdote records a professor who sat for hours reading papers. Then he rose and asked his neighbour to keep his seat for him while he went home for a cup of coffee. Vienna has been called "the mother of cafés" and it is possible that

CAFÉ
SCHWARZENBERG

the first "modern" coffee-house was founded there by the "patron saint" of coffee, Franz George Kolschitsky.

During the Turkish siege of Vienna in 1683, Kolschitsky acted as interpreter for the Turkish army which left behind sacks of green coffee beans when they finally retreated. Kolschitsky was able to prepare these and turn them into coffee as the Turks had done. He then hawked his coffee through the streets, as the American entrepreneur Pascal was to do in Paris.

For his efforts during the siege, the city authorities awarded Kolschitsky a house, which he turned into the first Viennese coffee-house, serving blended and flavoured coffees. Alongside each cup a crescent-shaped biscuit was offered, and still is, as a tribute to the Turks.

COFFEESPEAK

With the fashionable trend in coffee-drinking, which started on the west coast of America, has come a new "cool" jargon. For example, super-busy supermodel Linda Evangelista likes her Starbucks coffee "half-caf, double-tall, non-fat, whole-milk foam, bone-dry, half-pump mocha, half sugar in the raw, double cup, no lid, capp". And being so busy she "takes it flying".

Which put simply means she wants a large, not-too-frothy, mocha-blend cappuccino, caffeine reduced. The rest is self-explanatory. And she wants it to take away!

FRANCE

The first coffee purveyor in Paris was an American called Pascal. He employed waiters to advertise his wares, bearing coffee pots and oil-heaters through the streets.

However, the most famous coffee-house is the eponymous Café Procope, founded by François Procope in 1689. His elegant designs, including tapestries, gilt mirrors, marble tables and great chandeliers, made coffee acceptable in fashionable society. Situated opposite the Comédie Française, it also attracted a theatrical clientele.

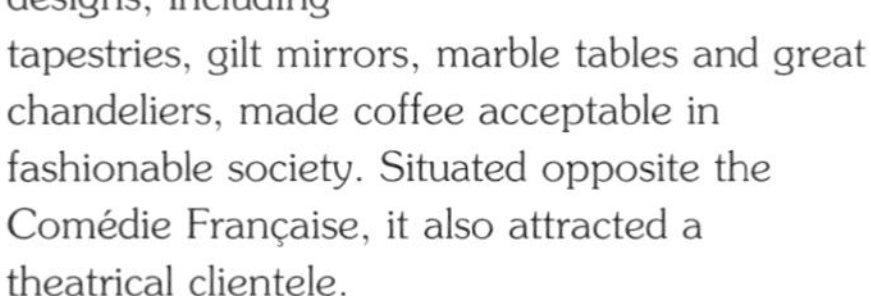

If in Paris, it is a must to breathe in the atmosphere of Parisian coffee-houses enjoyed by Voltaire, Rousseau and Beaumarchais, along with the revolutionaries, Marat and Robespierre. From coffee-houses such as these the typical French brasseries evolved and we can still savour coffee at Les Deux Magots, Café de Flore, Café de la Paix, and a host of others in Montmartre and on Boulevard des Italiens and la Madeleine.

GERMANY

No one city in Germany was linked to coffee, as the whole nation took to it in a big way in the late 18th century. Liberated women made the *Kaffeeklatsch* the perfect place to meet, to discuss everything from family matters to Beethoven's latest composition.

Coffee became a replacement for beer at breakfast, tea on family outings and the mainstay of many spacious cafés.

Instead of being accompanied by dainty crescents, German coffee is best enjoyed with big, big, portions of *torten mit schlagsahne*. Revel in excess!

ITALY

Perhaps the most famous coffee-house in Italy is Caffè Florian in Venice's imposing St Mark's Square. Opened in 1720 by Floriano Francesconi, at a time when Venice's coffee was said to be the best in the world, this is where Casanova used to take his daily infusion and where writers like Goethe, Dickens and Proust also savoured the wonderful aromas.

Caffè Florian still has that comforting mixture of intimacy and grandeur. The waitresses no longer give the gentlemen buttonholes, but ladies are still serenaded by

violin. This is the perfect location in early evening when the square empties of tourists.

Noted coffee lovers at the Caffè Greco in Rome have ranged from popes, starting with Leo XIII, and heads of state from Louis I of Bavaria, to Presidents Mitterand and Kennedy, and King Constantine of Greece.

Florence's young bloods frequent the Giacosa on the Via Tornabuoni. Not far away is Doney's, the traditional haunt of writers and artists since the early 19th century.

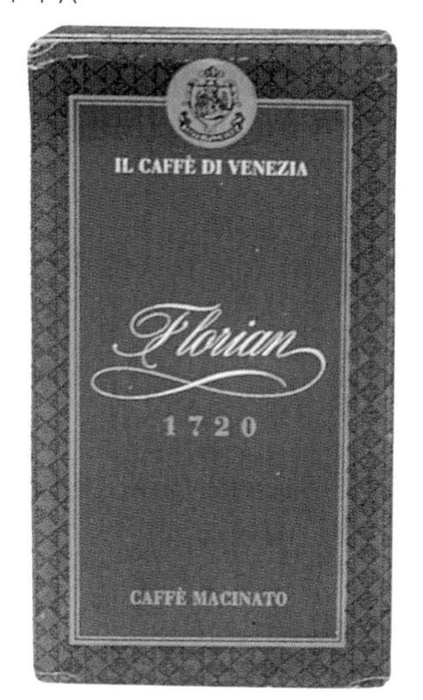

JAPAN

Like much of the world's finest food and drink, coffee has quickly found its niche among the smart set in Japan. In Tokyo's Minato-ku district, the Chianti has established a well-deserved reputation for its excellent espresso, served in the ground-floor coffee bar of this popular Italian restaurant.

In the same district, Stove Root evokes the easy comfort of a rambling American coffee bar, somewhere to retreat from the Tokyo hubbub to enjoy a cup of your favourite blend.

SWITZERLAND

Famed for its chocolate, Switzerland is also home to some long-established cafés. In Zurich the Café Schober on Napfcasse is a comfortable rambling café full of old-world charm and home to some of Europe's most delicious chocolate cakes. Students and seasoned veterans of café life, reading newspapers on sticks, rub shoulders here as they have done for generations.

With chocolate on the mind, Confiserie Sprungli at Paradeplatz on Bahnhofstrasse, produces some of the country's finest chocolates, among them its celebrated white truffles. However, it is worth a visit simply for its coffee and if you are feeling peckish, its restaurant is highly regarded as well.

GET POURING – THE WORLD'S TOP TEN COFFEE-DRINKING COUNTRIES IN ORDER

United States
Germany
Brazil
Japan
France
Italy
Spain
United Kingdom
Indonesia
Netherlands

GUATEMALA
HAWAI
MARAGOGYPE

ESTIMABLE ESTATES

Coffee Producers

"The morning cup of coffee has an exhilaration about it which the cheering influence of the afternoon or evening cup of tea cannot be expected to reproduce."
OLIVER WENDELL HOLMES, *OVER THE TEACUPS*

Although Brazil is the world's leading producer of coffee, the revival of interest in coffee has led discriminating connoisseurs to seek out smaller, but no less exclusive, producers.

Brazil's tropical climate makes the country the world's leading producer of coffee

BRAZIL

Famously, they have an awful lot of coffee in Brazil. With an estimated four billion coffee trees, Brazil produces around a third of the world's coffee today. Quantity comes before quality, making it impossible to define a particular Brazilian flavour.

Coffee grown on Brazil's northern seaboard has a tangy taste reminiscent of the sea. It is a popular flavour in the Middle East and North Africa.

Single-estate coffees to sample include washed Bahia, which has a refined taste, much enjoyed in America and Brazil itself. Others are Capin Bianco, which is very smooth, and Vista Allegro, which is spicy and brambly. Coffees such as these, like many wines from Burgundy, are often best drunk young.

COLOMBIA

Colombia is the world's second largest producer of coffee, after Brazil. Colombian coffees are consistently good, mild coffees, with a caramel flavour. The finest are grown in the foothills of the Andes, around 4,000 ft (1,220 m) above sea level. The most widely exported grades are Supreme and Excelsior. Other names to look out for are Medallion, Manzizales, Bucaramanga and Bogota.

COSTA RICA

Costa Rican coffees are high-altitude and therefore classic coffees. The "grand crus" are notable and include those from estates like Tarrazu, Tres Rios and Juan Vinas.

Only *arabica* trees are grown; growing *robusta* is actually illegal. Look out for the initials SHB, meaning "Strictly Hard Bean", grown at an altitude of 5,000 ft (1,500 m). Rich and aromatic, SHB is the hallmark of seductive flavours.

CUBA

The perfect marriage of coffee and cigars evokes the spirit of Cuba. And Cuban coffee often has a smoky flavour.

The 1792 slave rebellion in Haiti sent a tide of refugees to Cuba, taking their coffee-producing skills with them. Though grown at low altitudes, Cuban coffees have some of the characteristics of Jamaican coffee. Single-estate coffees to look out for include Turquino, which is said to be reminiscent of the style of coffee once produced in French colonies, such as Martinique and Réunion.

DOMINICAN REPUBLIC

High-quality coffee has been grown here since the early part of the 18th century. Names to look out for are Bani, Juncalito and Ocoa. Sometimes these sweet, but full-bodied coffees are labelled "Santa Domingo". They are ideal with a quick nibble during the day.

GUATEMALA

Guatemala produces some of the very finest SHB coffees, the most notable estates being Cobans, Antiguas and Heuheutenango.

The slopes of the volcanic mountains of the Sierra Madre provide perfect conditions for growing *arabica* coffee beans. In severe weather, fires are lit near the plantations to hold back the frost. They impart a smoky flavour in the process. Guatemalan coffees are best savoured with a post-prandial smoke.

HAITI

In spite of political problems, much high-quality coffee has been produced here since the Jesuits planted the first coffee trees in Haiti in 1715.

The flavour of Haitian coffee resembles that of the famed Jamaican Blue Mountain coffee. Indeed, the Japanese often mix Haitian and Jamaican to make the latter, more expensive, coffee go further.

Coffee production in Haiti is only now increasing, and the typical caramel taste of Haitian coffee is becoming popular around the world.

HAWAII

The Hawaiian Kona bean is regarded by many as the world's most beautiful coffee bean. Hawaiian coffee trees are grown in man-made depressions hollowed out of the lava rock on the slopes of Mauna Loa, a volcano in the Kona district of Hawaii. Hawaiian coffee, celebrated for its deliciously rich aromas, is complex, cinnamony and spicy.

JAMAICA

Jamaican Blue Mountain is synonymous with quality coffee and expensive quality at that.

Jamaica, like Cuba, was a beneficiary of the 1792 Haitian rebellion, though there are records of coffee being planted in Jamaica as early as 1730. The trees which now produce the distinctive blue/green beans are grown on small estates such as Silver Hill and Atlanta, where the mountainous terrain makes mechanization difficult.

Blue Mountain has long been a favourite coffee in Japan and in 1969 Japanese companies

There is a link between the altitude at which coffee is grown and its quality – the higher the plantation, the better the quality of the coffee it produces. Top-quality Kenyan coffees may be cultivated as high as 6,000ft (1,830m). The cooler air slows the rate of growth of the plants and allows the full development of flavour.

began investing heavily in the Jamaican coffee industry, with the result that the cream of the crop now goes to Japan. The fact that you have to use more beans per cup than with most other coffees also adds to its expense.

Most aficionados are happy to pay the high price Blue Mountain commands, in order to savour its simple, sweet and aromatic flavour.

KENYA

The Kenyan coffee industry is highly regulated to provide the drinker with a consistently good cup. In these days of serious coffee drinking the only slight complaint is that Kenyan coffee is pooled from lots of small-holdings making for a certain homogeneity. Perhaps some more interesting flavours, tailored to suit particular coffee "moods", might be achieved if roasters could buy beans from individual planters.

Some of the blends have an almost alcoholic quality, making them perfect night-caps. Others, with greater acidity, have excellent flavour and fragrance.

A medium roast is best, but the highest graded beans can be high-roasted. One unusual Kenyan product is the Kenya Peaberry coffee tree. This produces a distinctive round bean, which enables it to absorb the flavours of the berry to the full. The beans, in turn, make intensely flavoured coffee. Kenyan Peaberry coffee is sometimes called Chagga after the tribe which cultivates it.

MEXICO

Mexico produces fine coffees with mellow flavours. Estates to look out for include Caotapec, Oaxa and Chiapas. Their Maragogype is the best variety of *arabica* grown in the Central American region. Enthusiasts for organic produce will appreciate Mexican coffee, as few insecticides or other chemicals are used by Mexican coffee growers, who are generally too poor to afford them.

Mexican coffee typically tastes smooth and fragrant, and the beans are best high-roasted.

PUERTO RICA

Puerto Rico is not a big player in the world coffee stakes and can not rival its many Caribbean neighbours. Much of the coffee grown on Puerto Rico is used for home consumption, but what is exported is reliably aromatic.

TANZANIA

Tanzania produces fine coffees, not unlike those of neighbouring Kenya. Aromatic and sensual, coffee from the Kibo Chagga estate, on the cool, misty slopes of Mount Kilimanjaro, makes a cup of magnificent fragrance.

UGANDA

The equator passes through Uganda, giving the country a climate which has enabled it to become one of the world's main producers of *robusta* beans. They produce a full, rich coffee, which is often of sufficient quality that it is smuggled over the border into Kenya and passed off as Kenyan coffee. Most Ugandan coffee is produced by co-operatives, which makes it difficult to identify coffees from particular estates.

VENEZUELA

After considerable neglect during the 1980s, when most investment in Venezuela was channelled into the booming oil industry, Venezuelan coffee is back in a big way.

Fruity flavours, curiously sweet at times, complement heady aromas and mark Venezuelan coffee out as something quite different from those of its many coffee-producing neighbours.

This is a coffee to show off, especially when you can find a single-estate bean such as Montebello, Miramar, Trujillo (ignore the political connotations), or that of Jean and Andres Boulton from their estate in the Turgua district, near Caracas.

YEMEN

The Yemen produces coffee to savour, rather than drink for a kick, as it is low in caffeine. Yemeni coffee, called "mocha" after the port on the Red Sea from which the earliest shipments were made, is the product of a small bean, similar to the Kenyan Peaberry. It has light body and high acidity, but combined with exotic pungency. The hovering hint of chocolate in the flavour of Yemeni coffee established the habit of adding a dash of good chocolate to a cup of coffee.

ZAMBIA

Zambia produces excellent coffees, not unlike those of Kenya in both taste and price. Zambian coffee estates produce good blending beans, which makes some useful for that last cup before bedtime, while others, high roasted, are equally suitable for an early morning espresso.

ZIMBABWE

Clean, soft, fruity coffee has only recently been produced here. Small production makes it attractive to the gourmet end of the market, with family estates, such as Farfell Coffee, producing hand-picked berries and sun-dried beans.

A COFFEE TO DIE FOR?

The tiny, remote island of St Helena, in the South Atlantic, was once best known as the place of exile of the Emperor Napoleon, who was banished there after his defeat at the Battle of Waterloo in 1815.

Napoleon, understandably, had mixed feelings about St Helena. But having tasted the island's coffee he joined the ranks of its enthusiastic admirers and it provided one of his few pleasures in life until his death there in 1821.

Coffee has been grown on St Helena since the end of the 17th century, when the British East India Company planted seeds brought from coffee trees growing in Mocha, in Yemen. The coffee trees on St Helena today are their direct descendants, producing a rare, pure variety of coffee that has remained unchanged and untainted for 300 years.

Following a period of decline, the coffee plantations on St Helena were re-cultivated in 1987 and supplies of this super-premium coffee began to appear on the world market once again.

Blessed with wonderfully clean air and grown in almost completely organic conditions, St Helena coffee is now one of the most expensive and exclusive coffees available, on a par with Jamaican Blue Mountain coffee, with a price tag that can reach £25 (US$40) for half-a-pound (226 grams).

BLUE MOUNTAIN Top-quality Jamaican coffee.

BRAZILS *Arabica* coffee from Brazil.

CHERRIES Alternative name for coffee berries.

COFFEA ARABICA The Latin name for the coffee plant which came originally from Ethiopia.

COFFEA ROBUSTA Coffee originating in the Congo.

COFFEE The name is derived from the Arabic *qahwah*, Turkish *kahveh*.

KONA Hawaiian coffee.

MARAGOGYPE Brazilian hybrid coffee bean, also known as "elephantine".

MILDS *Arabica* coffees grown in countries other than Brazil.

ROBUSTAS Coffees grown mostly in Africa.

SHB Strictly Hard Bean, type of coffee bean.

SHG Strictly High Grown, type of coffee bean.